Desserts from Around the World

DiscoverRoo

An Imprint of Pop!
popbooksonline.com

COOKIES
FROM AROUND THE WORLD

by Grace Hansen

WELCOME TO DiscoverRoo!

This book is filled with videos, puzzles, games, and more! Scan the QR codes* while you read, or visit the website below to make this book pop.

popbooksonline.com/cookie

abdobooks.com
Published by Pop!, a division of ABDO, PO Box 398166, Minneapolis, Minnesota 55439.

Printed in the United States of America, North Mankato, Minnesota.

102024
012025

THIS BOOK CONTAINS RECYCLED MATERIALS

Cover Photo: Shutterstock Images
Interior Photos: Shutterstock Images, Alamy Stock Photos, Getty Images
Editor: Elizabeth Andrews
Series Designer: Laura Graphenteen

Library of Congress Control Number: 2024938595

Publisher's Cataloging-in-Publication Data

Names: Hansen, Grace, author.
Title: Cookies from around the world / by Grace Hansen
Description: Minneapolis, Minnesota : Pop!, 2025 | Series: Desserts from around the world | Includes online resources and index
Identifiers: ISBN 9781098247102 (lib. bdg.) | ISBN 9781098247669 (ebook)
Subjects: LCSH: Baking--Juvenile literature. | Desserts--Juvenile literature. | Baked products --Juvenile literature. | Cookies--Juvenile literature. | Confectionery--Juvenile literature. | Cookery--Juvenile literature.
Classification: DDC 641.8654--dc23

*Scanning QR codes requires a web-enabled smart device with a QR code reader app and a camera.

TABLE OF CONTENTS

CHAPTER 1

THE HISTORY OF DESSERT

Desserts can be traced back to ancient times. The Mesopotamians had a fruitcake-like recipe. The Ancient Egyptians sweetened round, flat breads with dates and honey and cooked them over hot stones.

WATCH A VIDEO HERE!

Much of what we know about the Ancient Egyptians comes from wall paintings in temples and tombs.

The shape celebrated the sun and moon. The Ancient Romans enjoyed simple sweet treats such as fruits, honey cakes, and fruit tarts.

This English oil painting from 1867 shows a first birthday celebration with cake and a candle.

DID YOU KNOW?

The word "cookie" comes from the Dutch word *keojke.*

In the 7th century, Persia (now Iran) was one of the first to harvest sugar cane and make cake-like cookies. In the 1500s, sugar became more affordable and widely available. In 1596, a cookbook was published for the growing middle classes in England. In it was a recipe for Fine Cakes. Later, Europeans made it more common to serve dessert, especially cake, for special occasions such as weddings.

Between 800 and 900, the Persians brought sugar cane to Southern Europe.

To this day, desserts help people around the world start the day, complete a meal, and celebrate important **milestones** and holidays. Let's go around the world and learn about cookies from different places and **cultures**!

Almond cake, such as the one in this Ancient Roman mosaic, would have required a great amount of effort to prepare.

Mochi has long been enjoyed in Japan to celebrate the New Year. It was said to harden the teeth and therefore extend life.

CHAPTER 2

COOKIES FROM EUROPE

Jammie Dodgers are popular English biscuits. They are made from **shortcake** and filled with raspberry or strawberry jam. The cookie, which was introduced in the 1960s, is named after the comic strip character Roger the Dodger.

LEARN MORE HERE!

Jammie Dodgers are popular packaged biscuits. But they can also be homemade!

DID YOU KNOW?

Hard or crisp cookies are called "biscuits" in the United Kingdom.

All kinds of fruits and nuts can be packed into Biscotti.

The word "biscotti" comes from the Latin *biscotus*, meaning "twice cooked." In Italy, many cookies are referred to as such. But in America, the word refers to the long, crisp, twice-baked Italian cookie. The first Biscotti were created in Tuscany in the 14th century. They were ideal for storing because much of the moisture was drawn out during the baking process. Today, Biscotti come in a delightful array of flavors.

Lemon pistachio is a popular Biscotti flavor.

MACARON OR MACAROON?

Macaroons are drop cookies made by adding shredded coconut to whipped egg white and sugar. Like Macarons, it is said that Macaroons come from Italy. Unlike Macarons, they are very simple to make.

The French are famous for their Macarons. However, the colorful cookies were first produced in Venetian **monasteries** beginning in the 8th century. When Catherine de' Medici moved to France to marry King Henry II, she brought Macarons with her. The sweet sandwich is **meringue** based and filled with **ganache**, buttercream, or jam. It is circular in shape and melts in the mouth.

Bakers can be as creative as they'd like with Macaron colors and flavors.

CHAPTER 3

COOKIES FROM THE AMERICAS

The Alfajor is a popular South American sandwich cookie. The Moors, who were a group of people from the Middle East, began to occupy Spain in the early 700s. They brought a small stuffed cookie called alajú with them. The Spaniards

EXPLORE LINKS HERE!

Baker Maria Rodriguez places dulce de leche to make Alfajores.

created their own version that they called the Alfajor. In the 1500s, the Spaniards brought Alfajores with them to the New World. People throughout South America began to create unique Alfajor flavors.

Alfajores can be dipped in chocolate or dusted in cinnamon.

Today, Alfajores come in many flavors throughout South America. The classic Argentinian Alfajores are made of two soft and crumbly cookies flavored with a touch of lemon. Between the cookies sits creamy dulce de leche. The cookie is coated in dry coconut flakes.

MEXICAN WEDDING CAKES

Much like Alfajores, the Mexican Wedding Cake finds its origins in the Middle East. The cookie also goes by different names in **cultures** throughout the world. In Mexico, the buttery sugar cookies, called *Polvorones*, are often served at weddings but are also popular during winter holidays.

There may be no cookie as classic or as **nostalgic** as the Chocolate Chip Cookie. Whether crunchy or chewy, dotted with chocolate chip morsels or packed full, the Chocolate Chip Cookie is a favorite of many. The most notable recipe was created in 1938 by American chef and baker Ruth Graves Wakefield. Her original recipe calls for Nestlé's yellow label semi-sweet chocolate.

Ruth Graves Wakefield was born in Massachusetts in 1903.

The Chocolate Chip Cookie has been dubbed "the American cookie."

CHAPTER 4

COOKIES FROM ASIA, AFRICA, AND THE MIDDLE EAST

Almond cookies are treats traditionally made by Chinese American **immigrants**. They are often baked to celebrate the Chinese Lunar New Year. They are buttery and have a deep nutty flavor. The cookies are meant to bring good luck and **prosperity** in the coming year.

COMPLETE AN ACTIVITY HERE!

Chinese Almond Cookie recipes often call for almond flour, almond extract, and slivered almonds.

DID YOU KNOW?

The Chinese Almond Cookie is shaped like a coin. This symbolizes good fortune.

Makroud el Louse, another delicious almond cookie, is from Algeria. This flourless cookie is made using sugar, eggs, and almonds. After the cookies are finished baking, they are dipped in an orange-flower sugar syrup and then tossed in powdered sugar. Most people enjoy them with tea or coffee.

Makroud el Louse is the perfect treat for anyone who is on a gluten-free diet.

Ma'amoul is a shaped, **fragrant** butter cookie that is famous in the Middle East. People of many **cultures** and religions, such as Muslims and

A baker carries a tray of Ma'amoul to prepare for the Muslim holiday Eid al-Fitr.

Ma'amoul shaped by mold can be very intricate.

Christians, enjoy them. Traditionally, the cookie is stuffed with date paste, pistachios, or walnuts. Ma'amoul cookies are often dome-shaped and topped with powdered sugar. The shape can be made by hand or by **mold**.

MORE COOKIES FROM AROUND THE WORLD!

1. **Mexican Cinnamon Cookies (Mexico)**
2. **Krichlate (Morocco)**
3. **Scottish Shortbread (Scotland)**
4. **Finnish Pinwheels (Finland)**
5. **Koulourakia (Greece)**
6. **Ful Sudani (Sudan)**
7. **Silvanas (Philippines)**

Countries and **cultures** around the world have their own unique and traditional desserts. Their ingredients and techniques can be similar to or very different from one another.

MAKING CONNECTIONS

TEXT-TO-SELF

Do you like cookies? If so, what is your favorite kind?

TEXT-TO-TEXT

Have you read any other books about food from around the world? What did you learn from those books that was not in this one?

TEXT-TO-WORLD

What are some other ways, besides dessert, that countries and cultures from around the world are special and different from one another?

GLOSSARY

culture — the language, customs, ideas, and art of a particular group of people.

fragrant — having a pleasant smell.

ganache — a sweet creamy chocolate mixture used especially as a filling or frosting.

immigrant — a person who moves permanently to another country from his or her native land.

meringue — egg whites beaten stiff with sugar and sometimes flavoring, used to form a pastry shell or as a topping on other baked foods.

milestone — an important event or turning point in history or in a person's life.

monastery — a community of monks, or the buildings used by such a community.

nostalgic — characterized by feelings of longing for a past time.

prosperity — the state of being wealthy and successful.

shortcake — a cake or biscuit made with a rich dough.

INDEX

DiscoverRoo! ONLINE RESOURCES

This book is filled with videos, puzzles, games, and more! Scan the QR codes* while you read, or visit the website below to make this book pop.

popbooksonline.com/cookie

*Scanning QR codes requires a web-enabled smart device with a QR code reader app and a camera.